FOREWORD

Did you know that there are over **30 billion dollars in unclaimed assets and over 1 billion dollars unclaimed in life insurance proceeds?**

This is because **family members don't know about or can't find all of their loved one's assets after their death.**

We tend to put off organizing our end of life affairs. This results in tremendous **added stress and anxiety for our loved ones** at a time of already high emotional grieving.

Did you know that an inventory of your **assets must be submitted to the courts within 90 days of your passing?**

This Book makes it **easier for your loved ones to fulfill their obligations to your estate.**

When you set aside time now to organize your affairs and commit your wishes to paper, **you are making it easier for your loved ones to cherish your memory** while settling your estate.

NOTE:

This book is for general information and does not cover all areas that may be suitable for your own circumstances.

This book does not substitute for legal, financial and accounting advice. We recommend you seek the help of qualified professionals for advice specific to your situation.

Making It Easier for My Loved Ones

ISBN 978-0-9852217-1-3

Copyright ©2014 by Focus and Sustain

Published by Focus and Sustain LLC
Kirkland, WA 98034, USA

All rights reserved. No part of this book may be reproduced or transmitted in any form or by any means, electronic or mechanical, including photocopying, recording or any information storage and retrieval system without written permission from the author except for brief quotations used in reviews, written specifically for inclusion in a newspaper, blog, or magazine.

DISCLAIMER

The purpose of this book is to educate and entertain. The author and publisher shall have neither liability nor responsibility for anyone with respect to any loss or damage caused, directly or indirectly, by the information contained in this book.

Printed in USA

www.focusandsustain.com

TABLE OF CONTENTS

My Story 5

Note to My Loved Ones 6

Instructions for My Final Rest and Memorial 7

Obituary Notice 9

Disposition of Personal Inventory 10

People to Notify 11

Organizations to Notify 12

My Key Information 13

Location of Key Items & Documents 14

Key Individuals 15

Key Professionals 16

Key Information for Bills and Revenue 19

Executor/Trustee Tips 20

Resources 21

Book Validation 23

Guidebook 25

<u>A small note as you begin:</u> You will find an asterisk (*) next to the items that are easier to fill in. Go ahead and start with them.

MY STORY

MY NAME:

*Honors I received:

Awards I received *(and what they mean to me):*

*Personal and Professional Achievements *(and what they mean to me):*

NOTE TO MY LOVED ONES

Share your love and appreciation of your family, your friends and your life:

☐ *See separate sheets attached*

If at any time you need help filling out this book contact us at **425-823-0984 x105**

INSTRUCTIONS FOR MY FINAL REST AND MEMORIAL

***Memorial Association Membership:**
Name:

Cremation
What I would like done with my ashes:

*Burial plot prepaid to or to be paid to:

Pallbearers:

Funeral
What I would like to wear:

What type of casket I would like:

My preferences on people viewing my body *(circle your preference)*:
I would like people viewing my body.   Y   N

My organ donation instructions & location of donor card:

MAKING IT EASIER FOR MY LOVED ONES©

INSTRUCTIONS FOR MY FINAL REST AND MEMORIAL

*Memorial service prepaid or to be paid in the following manner:

_____

_____

*Officiating religious or secular person(s):

Name: _____ Phone: _____

Email: _____

Name: _____ Phone: _____

Email: _____

*Service flower preferences:

_____

_____

Monetary donations can go to:

_____

_____

After-Service Gathering:

Location: _____

Type of food: _____

Beverages: _____

Who should say something: _____

OBITUARY NOTICE

I Want My Obituary Notice to read as follows or include the following information (see The Guidebook for ideas):

DISPOSITION OF PERSONAL INVENTORY

TANGIBLE ITEMS: ☐ *See separate sheets attached*

Personal Property Distribution Instructions:
Include jewelry, plants, books, photos, computer, furniture, art pieces etc. – see guidebook for ideas; Indicate use of and add separate sheet as needed:

___

___

___

___

___

___

PERSONAL ITEMS: ☐ *See separate sheets attached*

Personal Property Distribution Instructions:
What you would like done with personal letters, notes, journals, etc. – see guidebook for ideas; Indicate use of and add separate sheet as needed:

___

___

___

___

___

___

PEOPLE TO NOTIFY

***Name and Contact Information (Email Address or Phone Number) of all who should be notified immediately:**

***My Contact List can be found in:**

ORGANIZATIONS TO NOTIFY

***Schools and Colleges:**

_____
_____

***Military Service:**

Veterans Affairs ID #: _____

_____

Nonprofit Organizations, Community Organizations, Social Clubs, Professional Organizations

1. _____
   ☐ Executive Director   ☐ Board   ☐ Staff   ☐ Members
   ☐ Other *(please describe)* _____

2. _____
   ☐ Executive Director   ☐ Board   ☐ Staff   ☐ Members
   ☐ Other *(please describe)* _____

3. _____
   ☐ Executive Director   ☐ Board   ☐ Staff   ☐ Members
   ☐ Other *(please describe)* _____

4. _____
   ☐ Executive Director   ☐ Board   ☐ Staff   ☐ Members
   ☐ Other *(please describe)* _____

MY KEY INFORMATION

*Social Security #:

*Passport #:

*Driver's License #:

Post Office Box # and location:

Bank Accounts: ☐ *See separate sheets attached*

    Bank Name:

    Account Number:

    Bank Name:

    Account Number:

Computer Information: ☐ *See separate sheets attached*

    Login IDs *(or location of information)*:

    Internet Account/Server Information:

    Email Addresses/Passwords *(or location of information)*:

Cell Phone Information:

    Phone Number:

    Data Provider:

    Email Addresses/Security Passwords:

Frequent Flyer Mile Info:

Magazine Subscriptions:

LOCATION OF KEY ITEMS & DOCUMENTS

*Will:

Trusts:

Birth Certificate:

Passport :

Driver's License :

Marriage Certificate/Partner Agreement:

    Pre–or Post-Nuptual Agreement:

    Divorce Decree:

Social Security Card:

Keys:

Safe Deposit Box (location and location of keys):

Storage Locker:

Deeds of Trust:

Tax Return:

    Current Tax Return

    Prior Tax Returns

Private last letters to special people:

Certification of rights to control disposition:

Retirement Plan Information (pensions, annuities, etc):

Real Estate Titles (homes, timeshares, co-owned, rentals):

Financial Statements :

Auto Lease/Title/Registration:

Boat Lease/Title/Registration:

Stock & Bond Certificates :

Certificates of Deposit :

KEY INDIVIDUALS

***Executor / Personal Representative**

    Name:

    Phone: Email:

    Location of Instructions:

***Trustee**

    Name:

    Phone: Email:

    Location of Instructions:

***Guardians of Children**

    Name:

    Phone: Email:

    Location of Instructions:

    Name:

    Phone: Email:

    Location of Instructions:

***Guardian of Pets**

    Name:

    Phone: Email:

    Location of Instructions:

KEY PROFESSIONALS

***Attorneys:**

    Name: _____

    Phone: _____   Email: _____

    Name: _____

    Phone: _____   Email: _____

    Name: _____

    Phone: _____   Email: _____

***Accountants:**

    Personal Accountant

    Name: _____

    Phone: _____   Email: _____

    Business Accountant

    Name: _____

    Phone: _____   Email: _____

***Financial Advisors:**

    Name: _____

    Phone: _____   Email: _____

    Name: _____

    Phone: _____   Email: _____

KEY PROFESSIONALS

*Mortgage Provider:

Account #:

Phone: Email:

*Investment Accounts/Retirement Plans:

Name:

Phone: Email:

Name:

Phone: Email:

*Insurance Agents:

Life Insurance Agent:

Name:

Phone: Email:

Disability Insurance Agent:

Name:

Phone: Email:

Long-term Care Agent:

Name:

Phone: Email:

KEY PROFESSIONALS

***Insurance Agents:**

Home Insurance Agent:

Name: _____

Phone: _____   Email: _____

Auto Insurance Agent:

Name: _____

Phone: _____   Email: _____

Medical Insurance Agent:

Name: _____

Phone: _____   Email: _____

Renters Insurance Agent:

Name: _____

Phone: _____   Email: _____

Business:

Name: _____

Phone: _____   Email: _____

Property and Casualty (P&C) Agent:

Name: _____

Phone: _____   Email: _____

Other:

Name: _____

Phone: _____   Email: _____

If at any time you need help filling out this book contact us at **425-823-0984 x105**

KEY INFORMATION FOR BILLS AND REVENUE

Debts Owed to me:

   Name:

   Phone: Email:

   Location of Contract:

Debts I Owe:

   Name:

   Phone: Email:

   Location of Contract:

Credit Cards:

   Issuing Bank:

   CC Number: Payment Due Date:

   Issuing Bank:

   CC Number: Payment Due Date:

Unpaid Utility Bills:

   Name of Utility Company:

Sources of Income:

   Source Name:

   Account #:   Email:

   Location of Contract:

Business Interests Owned:

   Name of Business:

   Name of the Contact Person:

   Phone: Email:

   Location of Contract:

EXECUTOR/TRUSTEE TIPS

- **Secure home,** water plants, remove mail from mailbox, pick up papers from walkway.
- Take someone with you to **meet with the funeral director** to ensure they follow your loved one's wishes.
- **Make appointments with attorney, accountant, financial advisors and insurance agents to review your roles,** responsibilities, deadlines and locations of documents.
- **Mail: File change of address form; cancel subscriptions.**
- **Home security; notify Home Owners' Association.**
- **Obtain death certificate.**
    - » Get at least ten certified copies from the Department of Health in the jurisdiction where the death occurred or from the funeral director. You may need them to collect on life insurance contracts, transfer titles, close accounts, obtain benefits and more.
    - » Make an additional ten uncertified copies.
- Find a financial institution (i.e., bank or credit union) that can provide **signature guarantees for certain documents as necessary.**
- **Notify creditors and close accounts.**
- **List Items:** (Under current law, the Executor must file an inventory and appraisal of decedents' assets to probate court within 90 days following death).
- **Distribute assets as appropriate** within the creditor "run out" period.
- **File account with Probate Court** listing income to the estate since the date of death, and all expenses and estate distributions for final distribution.
- **Contact Employee Benefit Department** for potential death benefits to be paid out.
- **Change titles** to house, investments, bank accounts.
- **Restructure Insurance policies** as necessary.
- **Delegate, delegate, delegate.** There are family members and friends who want to help

If at any time you need help filling out this book contact us at **425-823-0984 x105**

RESOURCES

Funeral Consumers Alliance	www.funerals.org
National Funeral Directors Association	www.nfda.org
National Cremation Society	www.nationalcremation.com
Federal Trade Commission	www.ftc.gov
AARP	www.aarp.org
Social Security Benefits	800.772.1213
Department of Veteran's Affairs	800.827.1000
Bureau of Unclaimed Property	www.unclaimed.org

Please keep in mind the confidential nature of the information recorded in this book. It should be kept in a safe location, preferably locked, and accessible only by the people you fully trust. Let them know where this book is located and how they can access it at the time of your death.

BOOK VALIDATION

I, _____ have signed this book on _____ , 20____

This book is meant as a guideline and does not replace my will.

Signature: _____

Print Name: _____

Guidebook

For Filling Out
Your
**Making It Easier
For My Loved Ones©**
Book

Did you know that **there are $30 billion of unclaimed assets** held by state treasuries, the social security office, life insurance companies, even the Screen Actors Guild? Annuities, CDs, investment accounts, settlements, safe deposit box property, autos, tax refunds, lotteries, deeds, real estate, debts owed, and more have been left unclaimed by people just like you. How does this happen?

Every day executors/ personal representatives are called upon to settle estates of their loved ones. For many of these people, a nightmare unfolds at a time when their grief is high. They **don't know where any of the decedent's important documents are**. It's not because the beneficiaries don't want to benefit from the assets; it's because executors don't know these assets exist. Did you know that about 25% of life insurance policies are unclaimed by beneficiaries? **Don't let your assets go unclaimed.**

Imagine being an executor to a loved one's estate. You are filled with sadness and when you find that things are not organized, adding a sense of aggravation at all the time you now have to spend finding things and then a sense of guilt about feeling resentment. And during all this you have a fixed deadline to meet. Within 90 days of your loved one's death, you have to file a report with the probate court listing the inventory and its value.

Don't you wish there were something easy to fill out and have at hand, like an instruction manual to make it easier for your loved ones to benefit from at a time when their emotions are raw, their grieving is acute? Don't you wish you had a book like this when you were an executor?

Well you don't have to wish anymore. Now you have your own book. It is designed to make it easier for your loved ones to fulfill your special wishes when you are gone.

The book is designed to be **one of the greatest gifts you can leave your loved one**; an organized system of what to do, where things are, and who to contact when you are not physically there to help.

The book is **organized in such a way to make it easy for you to fill out personal and key information.** It also allows you to include extra pages of additional information. Most of all, the book is designed to serve as a guide for your loved ones. **They can fulfill their responsibility to your wishes instead of feeling distraught and anxious** about where all your documents, and important information and how you would like certain sensitive topics handled like your memorial service, or the disposition of your tangible items or how a pet needs to be cared for.

The book is the tool to tell your loved ones where important information like your passwords are located, all of your life insurance policies are, or who to contact from high school, college, places you volunteer, clubs you belong to and more.

Perhaps you have given these subjects some thought only to find that you've put those thoughts on the back burner...AGAIN. Well no more. The book is your expression to "Let Me Make It Easier for You when I'm gone."

Think about, just for a second *if someone had to find your passwords, for your bank or insurance information; where would they possibly look for them?* What if you had to do it for someone you loved? How difficult might that be for you unless they told you where these passwords and other key information were located?

Keep in mind that there are restrictions to accessing accounts but letting your loved ones know where the information is when they need it is a valuable time saver.

Or, what if someone else had to decide for you, who is to receive your jewelry, art, antiques, or photos? They shouldn't have to do that should they? What if you were an executor and had to make decisions for a loved one? It would be very difficult to know what they really wanted, what they promised to whom, when more than one person is saying they promised THAT ITEM to them.

What if someone had to find your important documents, the ones that, if not found would add to the unclaimed property? Imagine their anxiety as they wonder if there is one more document lying around SOMEWHERE. It wouldn't be easy for them would it?

This book does not replace your will. It does not act as a legal document. Instead it includes your notes to help your loved ones at what is thought to be one of the most stressful time in ones' life.

Before I walk you through the book, please keep in mind the following:

At any time, when you find yourself not completing the book, please give us a call at 425-823-0984x 105. Tell us where you are stuck. Leave us your name and phone number. Mention how you received the book to see how you qualify for our FREE supportive phone call. We will contact you to see how we can help you complete filling out the book.

Take the time NOW to fill out the book. You'll be glad you did. Once it is completed, put it in a **secure location, one that your executor can easily find and access.**

Now, let's go through the Making it Easier for My Loved Ones Book©:

THE FOREWORD - Page 1

As you read the information in the framed box you will find that it serves as a great reminder to what makes the book so valuable.

If you are giving the book to someone you love for them to fill out, like a parent, spouse, friend, or sibling, **you might read this text to them.** It can let them know just how important they are to you. If you are the executor, you can let your loved one know that filling out the book will allow you to focus on their memory in a dynamic and loving fashion. Instead of being pulled by anxiety and worry over whether or not they have found all your documents, contracts, and policies, they can fulfill your wishes calmly and with great respect and honor to you.

MY STORY - Page 5

This section allows you to describe honors, achievements, and awards you have attained or received in your life. This is a section to describe what these honors, achievements, and awards have meant to you. **Although you may want to trivialize honors, they symbolize merit.** What did these honors and achievements recognize you for? What did it mean for you to have been singled out for these awards? Write those answers down.

When others hear about your honors, ***it will add more richness and understanding of what you stood for*** and accomplished. Others will be pleased to know you even better when they are reminded of your honors.

Take the time now to write down honors you have received from school, college, clubs, cities, societies and organizations. For example you may have been honored with a Phi Beta Kappa key, years of service or contributions to an organization, political or community project. You may have been honored as a friend or family member. List your honors here. ***They contribute to the tapestry of your life.***

Awards are any tangible way you have been recognized for an achievement.

Write down your awards.

These are important to write down so your friends can look at your history and enjoy a richer understanding of your valuable life.

Your awards might include sports, education, career or professional, public service, society, clubs or family awards.

Achievements are the distinctions or projects that you have succeeded in. These achievements ***may have taken courage or skill*** to accomplish.

Take the time to write down your achievements.

They could include: being an artist, a writer, a principal or founder of a business, a parent/grandparent/great grandparent, developing a passion, being the first at something, injuries, diseases you overcame or battled.

Whatever your achievements, write them down. ***They tell YOUR story.***

NOTE TO MY LOVED ONES - Page 6

What would you like to say to the ones you love? Here is your opportunity to write it down on a separate piece of paper and add it to the book. ***Share your love and appreciation of your friends and family members.*** Let them know what they mean to you.

What is important about this? You can probably guess. This will create great meaning and value to those who read it. **They will cherish your words forever.** That's how important this is.

Some people **don't know where to start** on Note to My Loved Ones. If you find you are in that group, then **pick up the phone and call us at 425-823-0984 x 105. Find out how we can help you get this done with speed and ease.**

INSTRUCTIONS FOR MY FINAL REST AND MEMORIAL - Pages 7 & 8

Your final rest and memorial directives can be a very sensitive topic. But when the time comes for your loved ones to deal with this necessity, the raw emotions of the situation can make it hard for them to think straight. Disagreements can flare up among family members as to what they believe you wanted. It is best to write down and then share how you want to be honored. This will greatly reduce potential conflict at the time of great grief.

If you belong to any Memorial Association jot its name and contact information here.

You don't want your family to squabble over your internment or burial wishes. You don't want them to feel guilty, wondering if they are doing what you want done with your remains. Jot down what you would like on these pages. If you wish to be cremated, indicate where you would like your ashes to rest. Some have wanted them scattered over mountains, cast into the sea, added to the soil on their favorite hiking trail. Whatever you want, indicate your wishes here.

Alternatively, if you want to be buried, write down the names of the pallbearers you would like to have, what clothes you would like to be buried in, the type of casket you want, how you want your body prepared (for viewing or not) and your organ donation instructions.

What is important about doing this? These are decisions that have to be made quickly. Can you imagine how hard it would be for your loved ones to make these decisions when you aren't there and you haven't told them? It would be excruciating. In the meantime the funeral homes may substitute their views for your wishes.

Write your wishes down now.

A memorial will be held to honor, celebrate and remember your life. There are details that have to be considered for this event. When you let your executor know your wishes for this service, you will have made it so much easier for them to deal with the possible pressures coming from the providers, well intentioned family members and friends. Remember to indicate where and how to pay for your service.

Take the time to write down those who you want to preside over your service. Include your preference for service flowers and where you would like any monetary donation to be made in your memory and honor.

Describe where you would like your post-service gathering to be held. Indicate what type of gathering you would like. You might want people to be able to share stories about their life with you in a deeper and more relaxed setting with each other. You might want a festive atmosphere with your favorite games or music played. You might want to provide a certain type of food for your friends. Whatever type of celebration you want, indicate your wishes here. And remember you can always edit it. Just erase or white out what you wrote, write something else, date it and put your initials by your new entry.

And remember, if you are avoiding or struggling to fill out the book call us at 425-823-0984 x 105. Leave us your name and phone number and we will contact you to see how we can help you complete filling it out. Mention how you received the book to see how you qualify for our **FREE** supportive phone call.

OBITUARY NOTICE - Page 9

This may seem like a trivial page but it really is very important.

Have you ever read obituaries? **Many of them may have looked like this:**

"Peter R. Abbot, age 87, of Brier, Washington, passed away on 6/8/20XX. He was born in Wausau, Wisconsin, went to Northwestern College graduating in advertising. His career was as an advertising campaign manager. He and his wife, Betty moved to Brier, Washington when he was transferred by his company. He is survived by his wife, Betty, his 3 children, Pete, Alice, and Jack and 5 grandchildren, Grace, Roger, Carey, Ginger and Jesse. In lieu of flowers, monetary donations can be made to the Agricultural Institution of Wausau. Please sign the guest register at…" (and the mortuary's name and site is provided.)

And that's it. Well, **that is emotionally unsatisfying for those who read it.** That type of information doesn't say anything about Peter that keep and reminds others of the richness of his life.

Fortunately today, people are providing more insight into their lives for acquaintances and friends who live a great distance away to read and fondly connect with you.

Here is an example of a more dynamic obituary:

"Peter R. Abbott made his final hop to greener pastures yesterday. He passed on 6/8/20XX in Brier, Washington with the same spirit he had all his life, one of adventure, enquiry, and humor. As a child he loved to serve tea at his sisters' tea parties, always dressing up in a costume to add humor to their events.

He was born and raised in Wausau, Wisconsin. He was an award winning debater in high school. For a while he threatened his family that he would one day be elected President of the U.S. due to his award winning debates. But after his final debate in high school, he announced he was not going to be a politician. It wouldn't be challenging enough. Instead he joined a group of young men and women in the newly forming advertising industry. The best ad he said that he ever wrote was the letter to his wife, laying out the benefits of a third date with him. She had been reluctant to have that date because she didn't want him to know she liked him.

Pete and Betty were married for 56 years. He was very proud of his 3 children and 5 grandchildren calling them his wife's best ads. As he said, "Their outstanding characters far exceeded anything I could have come up on my own."

At home he loved growing vegetables. He was known for his exceptional knowledge of soil and vegetable growing best practices. His gardening was modeled by many in the northwest due to his unique irrigation system. He developed this system while studying at the University of Wisconsin, Madison. Even after he and Betty moved to Brier, Washington, he continued perfecting his irrigation process. As he liked to say: "There's nothing like a great harvest when you know how to water the lettuce, carrots and corn."

His sense of adventure, his love of family, friends, and strangers (who doesn't remember the time he brought home "the rancher") will keep his memory living on in all our hearts.

We will celebrate his life. You might even hear the rest of the story of "The Rancher which few know and all will appreciate. Pete, you were the best. And as you requested, your memorial service will be held at: The Logan Lodge. It's the nearest facility to a briar patch. Pete always said, "When my time comes, just send me back into the briar patch." Contributions in Peter's name can be made to the or the Agricultural Institution of Wausau. And ask his 3 children, Peter, Alice, and Jack and 5 grandchildren, Grace, Roger, Carey, Ginger and Jesse about the tea parties he had with them. It not only became a tradition, but evolved into a long tale that has become part of the Abbott family legacy. Betty, his beloved wife, who passed on three years ago will be happy to welcome Pete back with her. "

Why not create your final notice? It might cost more **but it is your last opportunity to allow those who read it, your relatives, friends, and acquaintances, to share your life for one more time.**

When you are not used to talking about your life, it may be difficult to write about it. ***If you find it is difficult for you, reach out to us at 425-823-0984x105. You'll be glad you did.***

DISPOSITION OF PERSONAL INVENTORY - Page 10

If you have been involved in settling a loved one's estate you know how challenging it can be. Everything has to be itemized. Everything has to be cataloged. **The executor has to file an inventory and appraisal of assets to probate court within 90 days following a death.** This can be very difficult to compile. By filling out this page, you will greatly reduce the stress that is inherent here.

Personal items and tangibles not bequeathed under a will, trust or other legal document have to be distributed. You may have heard of homes being raided after someone's death: missing jewelry, missing art work and books, missing china and favorite knick-knacks. You don't want this. **This is not the time to have your loved ones squabbling and your personal representative at odds with your beneficiaries.**

You can do so much to making it easier for your loved ones by paying careful attention to this page.

The first area to examine is the Tangible Items. This list will include property such as jewelry, books, furniture, musical equipment, sports gear, art pieces, plants, photos, and computers. Indicate who is to receive them or how you want them distributed.

Your Personal Items include property like journals, letters, notes and clothes. Indicate here where your personal items are located, who is to receive them or how you want them distributed.

There may be emotional and sentimental attachments to some of your property. This is perfectly normal. Unfortunately, at a time like this, when your remaining family and friends are experiencing great loss, the attachment they may suddenly have to certain items can create great squabbles by those who are interested in having the same item.

You may find that you don't know how to decide who gets what. If this is a difficult area for you to examine, **you may like the following idea.**

Ask your intended beneficiaries to select the items, on your list of tangible and personal items, which they would like to receive.

Collect their individual requests. Separate and allocate the items that are only requested by one person. Mark these items with that person's name or indicate on your list to whom these items should be distributed.

When more than one person is interested in the same item we like the following two approaches.

First: Ask the interested parties to express why they want the pieces they have listed. This can help you understand their motivations, intentions and appreciation of the item. From their explanation you can begin to sort through the items and divide them up appropriately.

Second: Give instructions to your executor to have all your designated beneficiaries prioritize on paper, as they go through your undesignated property, the tangible items they want. The items will be assigned according to their priority on everybody's list and following an entire procedure designed to keep emotions calm and relationships intact. Rather than get into it here, contact us if you would like guidance on this.

This provides **an orderly way of handling a delicate matter**. It does not show favoritism. People get at least most of what they want if not everything. It makes for a more harmonious conclusion to the distribution of your undesignated items.

Items can have very sentimental meaning to others and it is best not to leave it to an executor to know how to distribute personal items that have not been designated and more than one person wants.

If you find one of these ideas appealing but don't understand how to convey the idea to your executor, please contact us by calling us at 425-823-0984 x105. Leave us your name and phone number and we will contact you to see how we can help you with this section. Mention how you received the book to give you an immediate additional discount to our services.

PEOPLE TO NOTIFY - Page 11

You probably have a contact list of friends and associates, both personal and professional. Many, if not all, would like to know of your passing. **They will want to remember and honor you in their own way.**

Let your executor know where this contact list is and who should be notified immediately, and who should be notified later.

This becomes even more important when, like me, you have business contacts as well as personal ones. I remember hearing about a colleague of mine who passed on. The family was very grateful to hear of the story I added to the tapestry of his life. Because I was a business associate, they didn't know how their husband, brother, and father, influenced my professional life.

Let your executor know if you would like a memorial book at your service for people to add notes and photos.

ORGANIZATIONS TO NOTIFY - Page 12

Most people have schools, colleges, community organization, social clubs (book clubs, country clubs, networking or meet up type groups), non-profit organizations, and military organizations to which they are or have been affiliated.

There are people in all these organizations who know you, like you, and think about you from time to time. **They would like to know of your passing so they can remember and acknowledge you in ways that are meaningful to them.**

This page provides you with the opportunity for you to enter information of your various affiliations. With the information in here, your executor can now notify these institutions and societies of your passing.

Executive Directors, a representative from the military, a staff or board member, colleagues from clubs, organizations, and schools might want to send a remembrance note to your family or make a donation in your memory, or attend your memorial service.

MY KEY INFORMATION - Page 13

You have important information that your executor is going to need to settle your estate. Your social security number is needed to close your file. Your post office box number will ensure that your executor can access your incoming mail. Bank accounts need to be identified. Log in information, email addresses and passwords to accounts need to be identified. **Imagine what kind of extra aggravation and unnecessary time has to be taken when this information is not readily available.**

LOCATION OF KEY ITEMS - Page 14

Fill out this page so that your executor can locate your important documents. These documents may include:

- Will
- Trusts
- Birth certificate
- Marriage Certificate and any pre, post nuptial agreements
- Social Security Card
- Partner Agreements both personal and professional
- Divorce Decrees
- Keys to items like the house, the safe deposit box, the car, the jewelry box, the safe, storage lockers, and Post Office Box(s)
- Safe Deposit Box (s)
- Storage Locker

- Deeds of Trust, Tax Returns

- Private Letters to Special People

- Retirement Plan information such as pensions, annuities

Describe where documents like Real Estate Titles to homes, timeshares, co-owned properties, or rentals are located.

Describe where recent financial statements, pensions, annuities, investment accounts, retirement plans, CDs and tax returns are located. Remember you don't want to add to the $30 billion left unclaimed.

Don't forget to include the location of your car(s), car lease, boat(s), Title and Registration information.

Congratulations on filling all this out!!!!! You are making it so much easier for your loved ones to take care of your affairs. You are leaving them an immeasurable gift of time and ease by having this ready for them.

KEY INDIVIDUALS - Page 15

This page lists key people you have designated to oversee your will, trusts, children and pets. Be sure to include where the location of instructions and other documents essential to their responsibilities are located. Write down their names, phone numbers and emails.

If you want to **add a special note to any of these people you can clip your note to them to this page.**

Your note will NOT replace the instructions you have as a codicil to your will but it will provide a tip or special notation such as my second child especially likes to be read to at night while my first child likes to have pancakes on Sunday morning. This is meant to serve as a friendly note.

Clear instructions regarding your cat, dog, rabbit, bird or your other pet is helpful to your executor and family members who want to be respectful to your relationship with and proper care of your pets.

KEY PROFESSIONALS - Page 16, 17 & 18

These pages give your executor key people to contact as they sort through, make inventory of and catalog your affairs. Keep in mind, **your executor only has 90 days to file an inventory and appraisal of probate assets to the probate court.** Any items that have not been put into a trust would not be included here. Trust assets are dealt with differently and separately.

Write down the names, phone numbers and emails of your attorneys, accountants, financial advisors, mortgage providers, retirement plan administrators and insurance agents.

If a week from now, you find you still have not filled this out, contact us at 425-823-0984x105 or email grace@focusandsustain.com to find out how we can help you get this done.

KEY INFORMATION FOR BILLS AND REVENUE - Page 19

There is a lot for an executor to do as they settle your estate. Debts need to be closed out before your estate can be settled and closed.

You may have personal notes, business debts, or credit cards with balances owing.

Please write in the debts owed to you and debts you owe including names, phone numbers, email addresses and the location of corresponding contracts. Then write down the issuing banks of your credit cards, your credit account numbers and the payment due dates. Some institutions will keep billing you, adding fees and penalties if your executor does not contact them.

On the revenue side you may have a business interest that needs to pay your estate, income from an employer, a lottery winning, annuity, CD or bond provider, an inheritance administrator that needs to be notified. Include their contact phone and email information and any identifying account or contract number

Letting your executor know all this information **will help** them greatly **by providing them information they may not have even thought of looking for.** You are making the settling of your estate so much easier by filling this information out.

EXECUTOR/TRUSTEE TIPS - Page 20

Here your executor will find useful tips for them as they take on their important responsibilities regarding your estate and your affairs. This is not a complete list of what needs to be done. This merely acts as a nudge to remind executors of issues they may not consider on their own.

Because the probate court requires an inventory of probate-able assets within 90 days of death, your executor faces a deadline on certain responsibilities.

Your executor may find it very beneficial to talk to the attorney who drafted your will. They may find it valuable to talk to your financial advisors and accountants as they sort through your affairs. These professionals will be able to assist your personal representative more specifically with your estate matters in the time frames that they need to be attended.

When you lose a loved one, many emotions come up to the surface. *The sudden outpouring of grief is certainly one emotion that can make it very difficult to have to face the legal matters* that have to be sorted, some within fixed deadlines.

You are providing information that will relieve your executor/personal representative of hundreds of hours of searching and compiling information. You have saved them from feelings of guilt at feeling distressed while they are also grieving. You have saved them from anxiety when they want to focus on your memory. **You have given them a gift of love** and that gift comes in the form of ease. You have told them who to contact, where documents and key items are located, what your wishes are for your final rest as well as the distribution of your undesignated tangible and personal property. In essence you have created your own legacy by making it easier for your loved ones to carry on your memory with the dignity, respect, and honor your life provided them as you give them this book as a gift of love.

RESOURCES - Page 21

Here you will find a list of a few resources that you or your executor may find useful to have. Phone numbers or websites are provided for your convenience. Keep in mind that these websites or phone numbers may not be valid when you access this page.

Please read the words printed in the box. They serve to remind you to keep the book in a safe location, one that your executor knows about and is ***easily accessible after your passing.***

It would be terrific for you to **review this with your executor.** They would feel so much more at ease seeing the book filled out. It will provide an opportunity to ask questions or clarify any unclear directions from you.

BOOK VALIDATION - Page 22

When you have completed filling out the book, sign and date it.

Now put the book in a place that is safe and secure and easy for your loved one(s) to get to. Do NOT put it in a safe deposit box as your executor/trustee/ personal representative will not be able to access it until they can prove they have the authority to access it. This would be too late for many of your key wishes to be honored.

Your loved ones' grieving can continue unabated when they have this book. You have made it easier for them. **They will be grateful for your expression of love and caring** as they can fulfill your wishes, and sort through your estate much more easily than having to wonder, search, call, write, stay on long phone call holds trying to close out, find out, and retrieve benefits to your estate.

If at any time you need help filling out this book contact us at **425-823-0984 x105**

www.ingramcontent.com/pod-product-compliance
Lightning Source LLC
Chambersburg PA
CBHW081356230426
43667CB00017B/2850